ABT

FRIENDS
OF ACPL

Team Spirit

THE SAN FRANCISCO 49ERS

BY

MARK STEWART

Content Consultant
Jason Aikens
Collections Curator
The Professional Football Hall of Fame

NORWOOD HOUSE PRESS

CHICAGO, ILLINOIS

Norwood House Press
P.O. Box 316598
Chicago, Illinois 60631

For information regarding Norwood House Press, please visit our website at:
www.norwoodhousepress.com or call 866-565-2900.

PHOTO CREDITS:
All photos courtesy of AP Images—AP/Wide World Photos, Inc. except the following:
Jed Jacobsohn/Getty Images (cover); Topps, Inc. (6, 14, 20, 28, 34 right, 36
both, 38, 40 both, 41 all & 43); Black Book Archives (9, 30 & 33);
Bowman Gum Co. (21 both & 34 left).
Special thanks to Topps, Inc.

Editor: Mike Kennedy
Associate Editor: Brian Fitzgerald
Designer: Ron Jaffe
Project Management: Black Book Partners, LLC.
Special thanks to: Brian K. Aguilar

LIBRARY OF CONGRESS CATALOGING-IN-PUBLICATION DATA

Stewart, Mark, 1960-
  The San Francisco 49ers / by Mark Stewart ; content consultant Jason
Aikens.
      p. cm. -- (Team spirit)
  Summary: "Presents the history, accomplishments and key personalities of
the San Francisco 49ers football team. Includes timelines, quotes, maps,
glossary and websites"--Provided by publisher.
  Includes bibliographical references and index.
  ISBN-13: 978-1-59953-134-2 (library edition : alk. paper)
  ISBN-10: 1-59953-134-8 (library edition : alk. paper)
  1. San Francisco 49ers (Football team)--History--Juvenile literature. I.
Aikens, Jason. II. Title. III. Title: San Francisco Forty-niners.
GV956.S3S84 2008
796.332'640979461--dc22
                                                                2007007480

COVER PHOTO: The 49ers jump for joy after making a big stop on defense
during the 2006 season.

Table of Contents

SPORTS WORDS & VOCABULARY WORDS: In this book, you will find many words that are new to you. You may also see familiar words used in new ways. The glossary on page 46 gives the meanings of football words, as well as "everyday" words that have special football meanings. These words appear in **bold type** throughout the book. The glossary on page 47 gives the meanings of vocabulary words that are not related to football. They appear in ***bold italic type*** throughout the book.

Meet the 49ers

During the early days of **professional** football, the game on the field was a test of courage and a battle of brute force. Surviving a game was often more difficult than winning one! The San Francisco 49ers were one of the teams that transformed the *image* of the sport. They played a heart-pounding brand of football that used the entire field and focused attention on players with game-changing skills.

Win or lose, the 49ers have always been exciting. When everything is going right, they are almost unbeatable. When luck goes against them, they still have enough talent to win close games. They make football fun for their players and their fans.

This book tells the story of the 49ers. They are the oldest professional sports team on the West Coast, yet they always find a way to bring something fresh and new to the game. In a sport where gaining yards is everything, the 49ers know that standing still gets you nowhere.

Keith Lewis and Walt Harris jump for joy after an interception. The 49ers look for exciting players who make big plays.

Way Back When

In the years after World War II, professional football began to grow in popularity. Fans in many cities around the country wanted a team of their own. A new league called the **All-America Football Conference (AAFC)** began play in 1946. It placed teams in cities where the older **National Football League (NFL)** had not, including San Francisco, California. The 49ers were owned by two brothers, Vic and Tony Morabito, who ran a successful lumber company. The team was named after the pioneers who traveled to California after gold was discovered there in 1849.

The Morabitos signed a number of players who had been college stars in the San Francisco Bay area, including quarterback Frankie

FRANKIE ALBERT   Quarterback

Albert and receiver Alyn Beals. Buck Shaw, the team's coach, was from nearby Santa Clara College. The AAFC lasted four years. The 49ers finished second in their **division** each season to the Cleveland Browns.

Both the Browns and 49ers were invited to join the NFL in 1950. Over the next few years, San

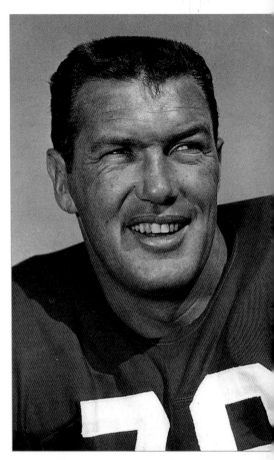

Francisco built an excellent team that included running backs Joe Perry and Hugh McElhenny, receivers Billy Wilson and Gordy Soltau, **linemen** Leo Nomellini and Bob St. Clair, and quarterback Y.A. Tittle. The 49ers won more often than they lost, but they never played for a championship.

The 1960s were not kind to the 49ers, but the team *regrouped* and played for the **National Football Conference (NFC)** championship twice in the early 1970s. Both times, however, San Francisco came up short. The 49ers had some good players, including quarterback John Brodie, receiver Gene Washington, running back Ken Willard, and defensive stars Charlie Krueger, Jimmy Johnson, and Dave Wilcox. However, it was not until Bill Walsh became the head coach—and Joe Montana became the starting quarterback—that the 49ers became a great **all-around** team.

In 1981, San Francisco won 13 games and defeated the Dallas Cowboys in a thrilling **playoff game** to reach the **Super Bowl**.

Montana then led the 49ers to victory over the Cincinnati Bengals. It was the first championship in team history.

The team won three more Super Bowls during the 1980s. The 49ers had several **All-Pro** players, including receivers Jerry Rice and Dwight Clark, running back Roger Craig, and defensive back Ronnie Lott. Other stars who took the field for the team were John Taylor, Keith Fahnhorst, Randy Cross, Jesse Sapolu, Keena Turner, Charles Haley, Tim McKyer, Eric Wright, and Fred Dean.

Steve Young became San Francisco's quarterback during the 1990s. He and Rice led the team back to the Super Bowl, with help from Ricky Watters, William Floyd, Brent Jones, Ken Norton Jr., Merton Hanks, and Deion Sanders. In January 1995, the 49ers won Super Bowl XXIX for their fifth championship.

LEFT: Joe Montana, the greatest quarterback in 49ers history.
ABOVE: Dwight Clark, an All-Pro receiver during the 1980s.

The Team Today

San Francisco plays in the West Division of the NFC with three very different teams—the Seattle Seahawks, St. Louis Rams, and Arizona Cardinals. The 49ers must have the skill and confidence to defeat these clubs, as well as the ability to reshape their game plan to match their strengths against the weaknesses of their rivals.

After winning their division in 2002 with a team of older players, the 49ers decided it was time to rebuild with a mix of youth and experience. In 2005, the team used the first pick in the **NFL draft** to select Alex Smith, a quarterback with the talent and attitude to lead the San Francisco offense.

The 49ers added more players that would help the team grow and succeed, including other young stars such as running back Frank Gore. The San Francisco defense, meanwhile, has been built around "playmakers"—smart, aggressive tacklers who increase their focus at crucial moments in a game. The 49ers always seem to find these special players, often after everyone else in the league *overlooks* them.

Alex Smith hands off to Frank Gore.
These young stars helped the 49ers rebuild their team.

Home Turf

For their first 25 years, the 49ers played in Kezar Stadium. It was located in Golden Gate Park, one of the city's loveliest parks. In 1971, the team moved into Candlestick Park, a short drive south of downtown San Francisco, on Candlestick Point. It was already the home of the San Francisco Giants baseball team.

Candlestick Park was enlarged for football, and its grass was replaced with artificial turf. In 1979, the 49ers and Giants agreed to switch back to real grass. Since 1995, the stadium has been renamed three times, first to 3Com Park, next to San Francisco Stadium at Candlestick Point, and then to Monster Park—after Monster Cable, the city's largest minority-owned business. Most fans just call it "The Stick."

BY THE NUMBERS

- *There are 70,207 seats in the 49ers' stadium.*
- *The 49ers hope to move into a new stadium in the city of Santa Clara in 2012.*
- *As of 2007, the 49ers had retired nine numbers—12 (John Brodie), 16 (Joe Montana), 34 (Joe Perry), 37 (Jimmy Johnson), 39 (Hugh McElhenny), 70 (Charlie Krueger), 73 (Leo Nomellini), 79 (Bob St. Clair), and 87 (Dwight Clark).*

San Francisco's stadium offers great views. This 49ers supporter is excited to face off against the Green Bay Packers and their famous "Cheesehead" fans.

Dressed for Success

San Francisco's *logo* was originally a California **prospector** (or "49er") firing two pistols. The smoke from his guns spelled out the team's name. In the 1960s, the 49ers began using a shield logo that was formed by the numbers 4 and 9. Their helmet logo, meanwhile, was an oval with SF inside of it. This design lasted for more than 30 years. The team uses the same basic logo today.

The 49ers' team colors are gold and a deep shade of red. Their original colors were a brighter red and silver. The team wore silver pants and red or silver helmets until 1964, when they changed to gold. In 1996, the 49ers switched to the deeper red. They also added black stripes to their jerseys. Today, they wear their dark uniforms for home games and their light uniforms for away games.

JOHN BRODIE
SAN FRANCISCO 49ERS

QUARTER-BACK

John Brodie wears the red and gold uniform of the 1960s.

UNIFORM BASICS

The football uniform has three important parts—
- Helmet
- Jersey
- Pants

Helmets used to be made out of leather, and they did not have facemasks—ouch! Today, helmets are made of super-strong plastic. The uniform top, or jersey, is made of thick fabric. It fits snugly around a player so that tacklers cannot grab it and pull him down. The pants come down just over the knees.

There is a lot more to a football uniform than what you see on the outside. Air can be pumped inside the helmet to give it a snug, padded fit. The jersey covers shoulder pads and sometimes a rib protector called a flak jacket. The pants include pads that protect the hips, thighs, *tailbone*, and knees.

Football teams have two sets of uniforms—one dark and one light. This makes it easier to tell two teams apart on the field. Almost all teams wear their dark uniforms at home and their light ones on the road.

Vernon Davis wears the deeper red uniform the 49ers started using in 1996.

We Won!

In 1995, the 49ers became the first team to win five Super Bowls. Their first title came 13 years earlier, in Super Bowl XVI against the Cincinnati Bengals. On that day, the 49ers relied on great defense and the passing of Joe Montana.

After San Francisco fumbled the opening kickoff, Dwight Hicks intercepted a pass to stop Cincinnati. The 49ers shut down the Bengals the rest of the first half. San Francisco finally surrendered a touchdown in the third quarter. When the Bengals threatened to score again, the 49ers got tough. Cincinnati closed in on San Francisco's goal line, but the 49ers stopped them cold on their next four plays. The final score was 26–21. Montana was named the game's **Most Valuable Player (MVP)**.

Montana was also the star in Super Bowl XIX, San Francisco's next trip to the big game. This time, the 49ers played the Miami Dolphins. In a battle between two great offenses, Montana got the better of Dan Marino, and the 49ers won

38–16. The Dolphins were ahead 10–7 in the second quarter, but Roger Craig scored two touchdowns and Montana ran for another to break the game open by halftime. Montana passed for 331 yards and three touchdowns, and once again was named MVP.

Montana's greatest game came in Super Bowl XXIII, in 1989. Facing the Bengals again, the 49ers trailed 16–13 with just over three minutes left. Starting from his own 8 yard line, Montana drove his team nearly the entire length of the field. He completed two long passes to Jerry Rice, a young star who had become his favorite receiver. Moments later, with the Bengals expecting another

LEFT: Joe Montana looks for a receiver during Super Bowl XVI.
ABOVE: Coach Bill Walsh gets a victory ride from his players after Super Bowl XIX.

pass to Rice, Montana threw a perfect spiral to John Taylor to win the game 20–16. Rice, who caught 11 passes, was named MVP.

One year later, San Francisco won its fourth title, against the Denver Broncos in Super Bowl XXIV. 49ers coach Bill Walsh had retired, and George Seifert was now calling the plays. The result was the same, however, as the 49ers won 55–10. Montana won his third MVP award.

The 49ers' fifth Super Bowl victory came against the San Diego

Chargers, in January 1995. On the third play of the game, quarterback Steve Young connected on a beautiful pass to Rice, who outran the defense for a 44-yard touchdown. Rice scored twice more, and running back Ricky Watters added a pair of touchdowns on the way to a 49–26 victory. Young set a Super Bowl record with six touchdown passes and was named the game's MVP.

LEFT: Jerry Rice dives for the end zone during Super Bowl XXIII.
ABOVE: Rice and Steve Young celebrate their victory over the Chargers.

Go-To Guys

To be a true star in the NFL, you need more than fast feet and a big body. You have to be a "go-to guy"—someone the coach wants on the field at the end of a big game. 49ers fans have had a lot to cheer about over the years, including these great stars …

THE PIONEERS

FRANKIE ALBERT   Quarterback

- BORN: 1/27/1920 • DIED: 9/5/2002
- PLAYED FOR TEAM: 1946 TO 1952

Frankie Albert was a master at hiding the ball from defenders. He would often fake two handoffs before throwing the football or running with it himself. Albert led the AAFC in touchdown passes two years in a row.

JOE PERRY   Running Back

- BORN: 1/22/1927
- PLAYED FOR TEAM: 1948 TO 1960 & 1963

Joe Perry was nicknamed the "Jet." The speedy runner could sprint through the smallest openings and was especially good on short screen passes. In 1953 and 1954, Perry became the first runner in history with back-to-back 1,000-yard seasons.

HUGH McELHENNY   Running Back

- Born: 12/31/1928
- Played for Team: 1952 to 1960

No runner during the 1950s was more exciting to watch than Hugh McElhenny. Once he passed the line of scrimmage, he made moves that left tacklers grabbing at air. McElhenny was nicknamed the "King" because of his amazing talent.

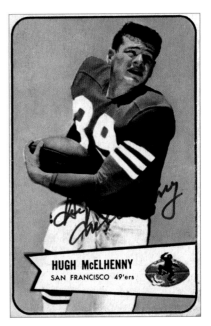

BOB ST. CLAIR   Offensive Lineman

- Born: 2/18/1931
- Played for Team: 1953 to 1963

Few players were scarier than Bob St. Clair. He stood 6' 9", was a savage blocker, and liked to eat raw meat. The 49ers also used him on defense when they made **goal-line stands** or wanted to block a **field goal**.

JOHN BRODIE   Quarterback

- Born: 8/14/1935
- Played for Team: 1957 to 1973

John Brodie might have been the most talented passer in the NFL when he played for the 49ers. His athletic ability stretched beyond the football field. After he retired, Brodie became a professional golfer.

LEFT: Joe Perry   **TOP RIGHT**: Hugh McElhenny
BOTTOM RIGHT: Bob St. Clair

MODERN STARS

JOE MONTANA   **Quarterback**

• BORN: 6/11/1956   • PLAYED FOR TEAM: 1979 TO 1992

Joe Montana was not built like an NFL superstar, but he was one of the

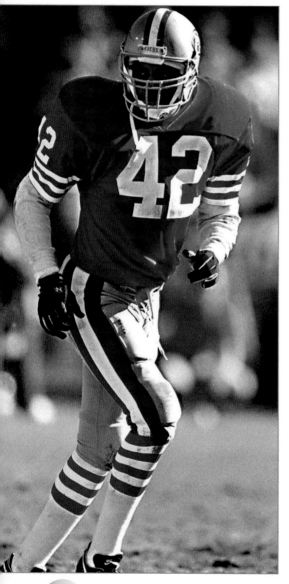

smartest and bravest men who ever took the field. He led the NFC in passing five times and guided the 49ers to more than two dozen fourth-quarter comebacks during his career.

RONNIE LOTT   **Defensive Back**

• BORN: 5/8/1959

• PLAYED FOR TEAM: 1981 TO 1990

When Ronnie Lott made a tackle, you remembered it. No one at his position ever hit harder. Lott was at his best when he played safety and was free to roam the field.

ROGER CRAIG   **Running Back**

• BORN: 7/10/1960

• PLAYED FOR TEAM: 1983 TO 1990

Roger Craig specialized in turning short passes into long gains. He was strong enough to run through tacklers and fast enough to run around them. He gained 1,000 yards three times and led the league with 92 pass receptions in 1985.

LEFT: Ronnie Lott   **TOP RIGHT**: Jerry Rice holds his Super Bowl XXIII MVP trophy.
BOTTOM RIGHT: Alex Smith

JERRY RICE   Receiver

- BORN: 10/13/1962
- PLAYED FOR TEAM: 1985 TO 2000

When Jerry Rice caught a pass, the play was just beginning. The speedy receiver could snatch a ball on the run and quickly shift into an even faster gear. When a defender tried to bring Rice down, he was also great at breaking tackles.

STEVE YOUNG   Quarterback

- BORN: 10/11/1961   • PLAYED FOR TEAM: 1987 TO 1999

Steve Young sat on the bench for four seasons waiting for his chance to replace Joe Montana. When his opportunity arrived, he led the NFL in touchdown passes four times and was the top-rated quarterback six times. Young was voted the league's MVP twice.

ALEX SMITH   Quarterback

- BORN: 5/7/1984
- FIRST SEASON WITH TEAM: 2005

When the 49ers used the NFL's top draft choice on Alex Smith in 2005, they believed he could lead the team the same way Joe Montana and Steve Young had. They were right. Smith later showed that he was a player San Francisco could build a championship team around.

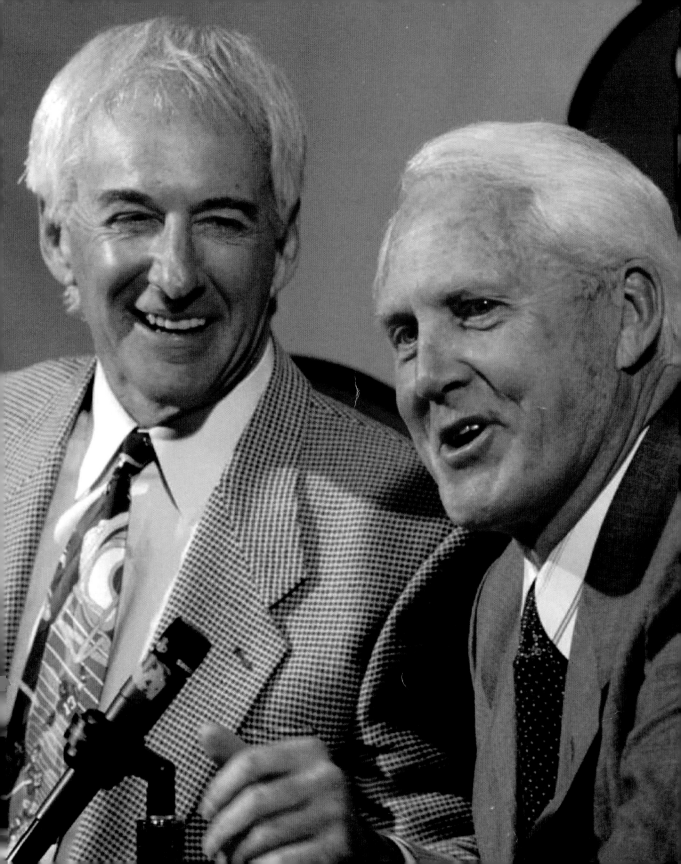

On the Sidelines

The 49ers have had some of the finest coaches in football. Three men—Buck Shaw, Frankie Albert, and Dick Nolan—each guided San Francisco to the *brink* of a championship. Shaw had a 71–39–4 record in eight seasons. Albert was coaching the 49ers when they fell just short of the 1957 NFL title game. Nolan built a team that came within one victory of the Super Bowl in 1970 and 1971. In 2005, the team hired Nolan's son, Mike, to coach the team.

The coach who finally took the 49ers to the Super Bowl was Bill Walsh. He believed that short, *precise* passing was the way to win. Walsh designed plays to create match-ups in the 49ers' favor and taught his receivers how to turn short catches into big gains. His strategy was called the "West Coast offense," and today almost every NFL team uses a form of it.

Walsh led the 49ers to three Super Bowls. George Seifert, Walsh's defensive coordinator, followed in his footsteps and coached the team to two more championships. Seifert was a 49er through and through. He had first worked for the club as an usher in Kezar Stadium in the 1950s.

George Seifert and Bill Walsh meet the press.
They led the 49ers to a total of five Super Bowls.

One Great Day

S an Francisco fans have long memories. When they took their seats in Candlestick Park for the NFC Championship game in 1982, they not only wanted to earn a trip to the Super Bowl. They also hoped to **avenge** three heartbreaking losses to the Dallas Cowboys a

decade earlier. The Cowboys had defeated the 49ers in the playoffs in 1970, 1971, and 1972. Now it was time for "payback."

The 49ers scored first when Joe Montana hit Freddie Solomon with a short touchdown pass. Before the opening quarter was over, the Cowboys came back to take a 10–7 lead.

The game seesawed back and forth all afternoon. Dwight Clark caught a 20-yard touchdown pass to put the 49ers ahead, but Dallas scored again before halftime to gain a 17–14 advantage. San Francisco reached the end zone in the third quarter to make the score 21–17.

Dallas responded with 10 points in the fourth quarter to lead 27–21.

The experienced Cowboys rarely lost in these situations, but they had never faced a Montana comeback. "Joe Cool" led the 49ers from his own 11 yard line down to the Dallas 6 yard line with a minute left. Montana called a pass play on third down, but his blockers could not stop the Dallas rush. The Cowboys chased him toward the right sideline as he looked frantically for an open teammate.

At the very last instant, Montana floated the ball toward the back of the end zone. He was throwing to a spot that only he and Clark knew about. They had run this "blind" play in practice many times and saved it just for these situations. Clark leapt high and snared the ball, landing with both feet inbounds.

Forever after, this play would be known as "The Catch." Ray Wersching's **extra point** gave San Francisco a 28–27 victory. It signaled the end of the Dallas *dynasty* and the beginning of the 49ers' glory years.

LEFT: Joe Montana drops back to throw a pass against the Cowboys.
ABOVE: Dwight Clark stretches for "The Catch" that sent San Francisco to its first Super Bowl.

Legend Has It

Who was the greatest two-way player in 49ers history?

Leo Nomellini
TACKLE   SAN FRANCISCO 49ers

LEGEND HAS IT that Leo Nomellini was. During his amazing career as a lineman with the 49ers, Nomellini was voted **All-NFL** on offense twice and on defense four times. Nicknamed "The Lion," he also may have been the toughest player ever to wear a San Francisco uniform. In 14 seasons, Nomellini never missed a single game, playing in 266 in a row. Teammates and opponents called him *indestructible*. Not bad for someone who did not play in his first football game until after he graduated from high school!

ABOVE: Leo Nomellini
RIGHT: Bill Walsh in disguise as a bellhop before Super Bowl XVI.

Who was the most feared tackler in football?

LEGEND HAS IT that Hardy Brown was. Brown was a linebacker for the 49ers from 1951 to 1955. Though he was small and slow, he hit opponents with such tremendous force that they often had to be carried off the field. Brown would crouch just before tackling the ball carrier, then "spring" into the player's upper body, using his shoulder as a battering ram. He was at his best covering punts and kickoffs. "Ball carriers avoided him like the *plague*," teammate Gordy Soltau once said. "He was something!"

Which 49ers coach also worked as a hotel bellhop?

LEGEND HAS IT that Bill Walsh did. Prior to Super Bowl XVI, Walsh disguised himself as a bellhop and offered to help the players with their luggage as they stepped off the team bus. He was hoping the joke would get his 49ers in a good mood and ready

for their game. It worked. San Francisco beat the Cincinnati Bengals 26–21.

It Really Happened

When did the 49ers become a championship team? A lot of fans think it happened in 1980—when the team finished with a record of 6–10! They point to a December game against the New Orleans Saints, when San Francisco went into the locker room at halftime trailing 35–7. The Saints had already gained more than 300 yards. The 49ers had only 21 yards.

No team had ever won a game when it trailed by 28 points. But no team had ever had a player like Joe Montana. It was only his third week as the team's starting quarterback, but he was no stranger to comebacks. In college, he had been known for leading his team to amazing victories.

In the second half against the Saints, Montana led the 49ers on four long touchdown **drives**. He ran for one score, passed for two, and handed off to Lenvil Elliott for the game-tying touchdown with under two minutes to play. New Orleans could not score at all in the second half, so the game went into overtime tied 35–35.

Midway through the extra period, Montana got the 49ers close enough to try a field goal. Ray Wersching kicked it

through the uprights for a historic 38–35 victory. It was the first of 26 fourth-quarter comebacks that Montana would lead for San Francisco.

"This was at the beginning for us," he said years later. "It really built our confidence."

LEFT: Joe Montana, master of the comeback.   **ABOVE**: Montana holds for Ray Wersching, whose overtime field goal beat the Saints in 1980.

Team Spirit

The 49ers are San Francisco's oldest major professional sports team. They draw fans from the city and its surrounding *suburbs*. Many families have been attending 49ers games for more than 50 years. The city loves a winner—players from San Francisco's five Super Bowl champions are still treated like kings when they come to games.

Prior to kickoff, thousands of fans hold wonderful tailgating parties in the stadium parking lot. Many also visit the 49ers Faithful City, which opened in 2006. There they kick field goals and test their passing accuracy, and also get to meet great players from the team's past.

During games, the fans are entertained by the Gold Rush cheerleaders, who have been performing since 1983. They were one of the first dance teams in the NFL. Also roaming the sidelines for the 49ers is their team mascot, Sourdough Sam. San Francisco is famous for its sourdough bread, which is how this 1849-style gold miner got his nickname.

LEFT: 49ers fans know how to make themselves heard.
ABOVE: Hugh McElhenny is one of many former stars who draw big crowds when they come to games.

Timeline

In this timeline, each Super Bowl is listed under the year it was played. Remember that the Super Bowl is held early in the year and is actually part of the previous season. For example, Super Bowl XLI was played on February 4th, 2007, but it was the championship of the 2006 NFL season.

1946
The 49ers finish 9–5 in their first season.

1970
Gene Washington leads the NFL with 1,100 receiving yards.

1949
The 49ers play in the AAFC Championship.

1954
Joe Perry leads the NFL in rushing for the second year in a row.

1962
Abe Woodson is the NFL's top **kickoff returner** for the third year in a row.

Buck Shaw, the first coach of the 49ers.

Abe Woodson

Terrell Owens
and Jerry Rice

Frank
Gore

1987
Jerry Rice catches 22 touchdown passes to set a new NFL record.

1995
The 49ers win Super Bowl XXIX for their fifth championship.

2007
Frank Gore represents the team in the **Pro Bowl**.

1982
The 49ers win Super Bowl XVI for their first championship.

1992
Steve Young is named NFL MVP.

2002
Terrell Owens leads the NFL in touchdown catches for the second year in a row.

Steve Young scrambles for a big gain during the 1992 season.

Fun Facts

ALLEY–OOP

The most famous pass play of the 1950s was the 49ers' "Alley-Oop." Quarterback Y.A. Tittle would throw a high pass to teammate R.C. Owens, a former basketball star who stood 6' 3" and was the best jumper in the NFL. He would soar a foot above the defensive players to catch the ball.

R. C. OWENS
END-HALFBACK   SAN FRANCISCO 49'ERS

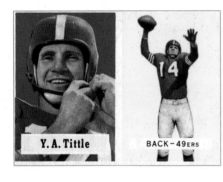

Y. A. Tittle   BACK–49ers

MR. COURAGEOUS

A great leader lifts his team's spirits and sets an example with the excellence of his play. In recent years, no one on the 49ers showed this type of leadership more than the team's brilliant defensive lineman, Bryant Young. Each season, the team hands out the Len Eshmont Award for courage and *inspirational* play. Young won it more often than any other 49er.

WINNING NUMBER

The 49ers were the only team in the NFL to win 100 games during the 1980s. They won 104, lost 47, and tied one.

BLOCK THAT KICK!

In 1956, Bob St. Clair blocked 10 kicks in 12 games. The 6' 9" lineman was a master at getting a hand on field goals and extra points.

MAD HOPS

The fastest 49er in history may have been Renaldo "Skeets" Nehemiah, who wore a San Francisco uniform in the 1980s. He owned many world records in the hurdles when he joined the team.

MILLION-DOLLAR BACKFIELD

In 1954, the 49ers had four future **Hall of Famers** in their backfield—quarterback Y.A. Tittle and running backs Joe Perry, Hugh McElhenny, and John Henry Johnson. They combined for almost 5,000 total yards of offense.

LEFT: Y.A. Tittle and R.C. Owens, San Francisco's "Alley-Oop" teammates.
ABOVE: Renaldo Nehemiah during his days as a track star.

Talking Football

"The 49ers were one heck of a football team. Everybody in the league feared us."

—Gordy Soltau, on the 49ers in their early years

"Success breeds success ... one or two bad breaks or incidents don't affect a team that's winning."

—John Brodie, on what makes a good team even better

"We were like one big, happy family ... I was part of that family."

—Joe Perry, on being the only African-American on the team in the 1940s

"It gave us a bright outlook for the rest of our careers. You could almost say it *made* our careers."

—Joe Montana, on the 49ers' first Super Bowl victory

"Competing against yourself—it's about self-improvement, about being better than you were the day before."

—*Steve Young, on what it takes to be an NFL star*

"This is the dream of almost every kid."

—*Alex Smith, on becoming the starting quarterback of the 49ers*

LEFT: John Brodie   **ABOVE**: Steve Young

For the Record

The great 49ers teams and players have left their marks on the record books. These are the "best of the best" …

49ERS AWARD WINNERS

WINNER	AWARD	YEAR
Billy Wilson	Pro Bowl MVP	1955
Hugh McElhenny	Pro Bowl Offensive MVP	1958
John Brodie	NFL Most Valuable Player	1970
Bruce Taylor	NFL Defensive Rookie of the Year*	1970
Bill Walsh	NFL Coach of the Year	1981
Joe Montana	Super Bowl XVI MVP	1982
Joe Montana	Super Bowl XIX MVP	1985
Jerry Rice	NFL Offensive Player of the Year	1987
Roger Craig	NFL Offensive Player of the Year	1988
Joe Montana	NFL Offensive Player of the Year	1989
Joe Montana	NFL Most Valuable Player	1989
Jerry Rice	Super Bowl XXIII MVP	1989
Joe Montana	NFL Most Valuable Player	1990
Joe Montana	Super Bowl XXIV MVP	1990
Steve Young	NFL Offensive Player of the Year	1992
Steve Young	NFL Most Valuable Player	1992
Dana Stubblefield	NFL Defensive Rookie of the Year	1993
Jerry Rice	NFL Offensive Player of the Year	1993
Deion Sanders	NFL Defensive Player of the Year	1994
Steve Young	NFL Most Valuable Player	1994
Steve Young	Super Bowl XXIX MVP	1995
Jerry Rice	Pro Bowl MVP	1996
Dana Stubblefield	NFL Defensive Player of the Year	1997
Bryant Young	NFL Comeback Player of the Year	1999
Garrison Hearst	NFL Comeback Player of the Year	2001

An award given to the league's best player in his first season.

Jerry Rice

Roger Craig

49ERS ACHIEVEMENTS

ACHIEVEMENT	YEAR
NFC West Champions	1970
NFC West Champions	1971
NFC West Champions	1972
NFC West Champions	1981
NFC Champions	1981
Super Bowl XVI Champions	1981*
NFC West Champions	1983
NFC West Champions	1984
NFC Champions	1984
Super Bowl XIX Champions	1984
NFC West Champions	1986
NFC West Champions	1987
NFC West Champions	1988
NFC Champions	1988
Super Bowl XXIII Champions	1988
NFC West Champions	1989
NFC Champions	1989
Super Bowl XXIV Champions	1989
NFC West Champions	1990
NFC West Champions	1992
NFC West Champions	1993
NFC West Champions	1994
NFC Champions	1994
Super Bowl XXIX Champions	1994
NFC West Champions	1995
NFC West Champions	1997
NFC West Champions	2002

** Super Bowls are played early the following year,
 but the game is counted as the championship of this season.*

Jimmy
JOHNSON
SAN FRAN. 49ERS ● DEF. BACK

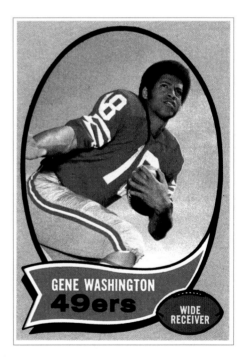

GENE WASHINGTON
49ers
WIDE RECEIVER

DAVE WILCOX ● LB

Jimmy Johnson, Gene Washington, and Dave Wilcox, stars for the 49ers when they won the NFC West from 1970 to 1972.

Pinpoints

The history of a football team is made up of many smaller stories. These stories take place all over the map—not just in the city a team calls "home." Match the pushpins on these maps to the Team Facts and you will begin to see the story of the 49ers unfold!

TEAM FACTS

1 San Francisco, California—*The 49ers have played here since 1946.*

2 Los Angeles, California—*Bill Walsh was born here.*

3 Seattle, Washington—*Alex Smith was born here.*

4 Albuquerque, New Mexico—*Ronnie Lott was born here.*

5 Dallas, Texas—*Jimmy Johnson was born here.*

6 Crawford, Mississippi—*Jerry Rice was born here.*

7 Chicago Heights, Illinois—*Bryant Young was born here.*

8 New Eagle, Pennsylvania—*Joe Montana was born here.*

9 Richmond, Virginia—*Ken Willard was born here.*

10 Brooklyn, New York—*Randy Cross was born here.*

11 Laie, Western Samoa—*Jesse Sapolu was born here.*

12 Lucca, Italy—*Leo Nomellini was born here.*

Randy Cross

43

Play Ball

Football is a sport played by two teams on a field that is 100 yards long. The game is divided into four 15-minute quarters. Each team must have 11 players on the field at all times. The group that has the ball is called the offense. The group trying to keep the offense from moving the ball forward is called the defense.

A football game is made up of a series of "plays." Each play starts and ends with a referee's signal. A play begins when the center snaps the ball between his legs to the quarterback. The quarterback then gives the ball to a teammate, throws (or "passes") the ball to a teammate, or runs with the ball himself. The job of the defense is to tackle the player with the ball or stop the quarterback's pass. A play ends when the ball (or player holding the ball) is "down." The offense must move the ball forward at least 10 yards every four downs. If it fails to do so, the other team is given the ball. If the offense has not made 10 yards after three downs—and does not want to risk losing the ball—it can kick (or "punt") the ball to make the other team start from its own end of the field.

At each end of a football field is a goal line, which divides the field from the end zone. A team must run or pass the ball over the goal line to score a touchdown, which counts for six points. After scoring a touchdown, a team can try a short kick for one "extra point," or try again to run or pass across the goal line for two points. Teams can score three points from anywhere on the field by kicking the ball between the goalposts. This is called a field goal.

The defense can score two points if it tackles a player while he is in his own end zone. This is called a safety. The defense can also score points by taking the ball away from the offense and crossing the opposite goal line for a touchdown. The team with the most points after 60 minutes is the winner.

Football may seem like a very hard game to understand, but the more you play and watch football, the more "little things" you are likely to notice. The next time you are at a game, look for these plays:

PLAY LIST

BLITZ—A play where the defense sends extra tacklers after the quarterback. If the quarterback sees a blitz coming, he passes the ball quickly. If he does not, he can end up at the bottom of a very big pile!

DRAW—A play where the offense pretends it will pass the ball, and then gives it to a running back. If the offense can "draw" the defense to the quarterback and his receivers, the running back should have lots of room to run.

FLY PATTERN—A play where a team's fastest receiver is told to "fly" past the defensive backs for a long pass. Many long touchdowns are scored on this play.

SQUIB KICK—A play where the ball is kicked a short distance on purpose. A squib kick is used when the team kicking off does not want the other team's fastest player to catch the ball and run with it.

SWEEP—A play where the ball carrier follows a group of teammates moving sideways to "sweep" the defense out of the way. A good sweep gives the runner a chance to gain a lot of yards before he is tackled or forced out of bounds.

Glossary

FOOTBALL WORDS TO KNOW

ALL-AMERICA FOOTBALL CONFERENCE (AAFC)—The professional league that played for four seasons, from 1946 to 1949.

ALL-AROUND—Good at many different parts of the game.

ALL-NFL—An honor given to the best players at each position in the early days of the National Football League. Today these players are recognized as being All-Pro.

ALL-PRO—An honor given to the best players at their position at the end of each season.

DIVISION—A group of teams (within a league) that all play in the same part of the country.

DRIVES—Series of plays by the offense that "drive" the defense back toward its own goal line.

EXTRA POINT—A kick worth one point attempted after a touchdown.

FIELD GOAL—A goal from the field, kicked over the crossbar and between the goalposts. A field goal is worth three points.

GOAL-LINE STANDS—Attempts by the defense to stop an opponent that is very close to the goal line.

HALL OF FAMERS—Players who have been honored as being among the greatest ever and are enshrined in the Pro Football Hall of Fame.

KICKOFF RETURNER—A player selected by his team to catch kickoffs and run them back.

LINEMEN—Players who begin each down crouched at the line of scrimmage.

MOST VALUABLE PLAYER (MVP)—The award given each year to the league's best player; also given to the best player in the Super Bowl and Pro Bowl.

NATIONAL FOOTBALL CONFERENCE (NFC)—One of two groups of teams that make up the National Football League. The winner of the NFC plays the winner of the American Football Conference (AFC) in the Super Bowl.

NATIONAL FOOTBALL LEAGUE (NFL)—The league that started in 1920 and is still operating today.

NFL DRAFT—The annual meeting at which teams take turns choosing the best players in college.

PLAYOFF GAME—A game played after the season to determine which teams play for the championship.

PRO BOWL—The NFL's all-star game, played after the Super Bowl.

PROFESSIONAL—A player or team that plays a sport for money. College players are not paid, so they are considered "amateurs."

SUPER BOWL—The championship of football, played between the winners of the NFC and AFC.

OTHER WORDS TO KNOW

AVENGE—To punish for a past insult or defeat.

BRINK—The very edge.

DECADE—A period of 10 years; also, a specific 10-year period, such as the 1950s.

DYNASTY—A series of rulers from the same family or team.

IMAGE—Appearance to the outside world.

INDESTRUCTIBLE—Impossible to wear down.

INSPIRATIONAL—Giving positive and confident feelings to others.

LOGO—A symbol or design that represents a company or team.

OVERLOOKS—Fails to see or notice.

PLAGUE—A deadly disease.

PRECISE—Accurate or exact.

PROSPECTOR—Someone who explores for gold and other minerals.

REGROUPED—Became organized in order to make a fresh start.

SUBURBS—Communities surrounding a major city.

TAILBONE—The bone that protects the base of the spine.

Places to Go

ON THE ROAD

SAN FRANCISCO 49ERS
490 Jamestown Avenue
San Francisco, California 94124
(408) 562-4949

THE PRO FOOTBALL HALL OF FAME
2121 George Halas Drive NW
Canton, Ohio 44708
(330) 456-8207

ON THE WEB

THE NATIONAL FOOTBALL LEAGUE   www.nfl.com
  • *Learn more about the National Football League*

THE SAN FRANCISCO 49ERS   www.sf49ers.com
  • *Learn more about the San Francisco 49ers*

THE PRO FOOTBALL HALL OF FAME   www.profootballhof.com
  • *Learn more about football's greatest players*

ON THE BOOKSHELF

To learn more about the sport of football, look for these books at your library or bookstore:

  • Fleder, Rob–Editor. *The Football Book*. New York, NY: Sports Illustrated Books, 2005.

  • Kennedy, Mike. *Football*. Danbury, CT: Franklin Watts, 2003.

  • Savage, Jeff. *Play by Play Football*. Minneapolis, MN: Lerner Sports, 2004.

Index

The Team

MARK STEWART has written more than 20 books on football, and over 100 sports books for kids. He grew up in New York City during the 1960s rooting for the Giants and Jets, and now takes his two daughters, Mariah and Rachel, to watch them play in their home state of New Jersey. Mark comes from a family of writers. His grandfather was Sunday Editor of *The New York Times* and his mother was Articles Editor of *The Ladies' Home Journal* and *McCall's*. Mark has profiled hundreds of athletes over the last 20 years. He has also written several books about New York and New Jersey. Mark is a graduate of Duke University, with a degree in History. He lives with his daughters and wife Sarah overlooking Sandy Hook, New Jersey.

JASON AIKENS is the Collections Curator at the Pro Football Hall of Fame. He is responsible for the preservation of the Pro Football Hall of Fame's collection of artifacts and memorabilia and obtaining new donations of memorabilia from current players and NFL teams. Jason has a Bachelor of Arts in History from Michigan State University and a Master's in History from Western Michigan University where he concentrated on sports history. Jason has been working for the Pro Football Hall of Fame since 1997; before that he was an intern at the College Football Hall of Fame. Jason's family has roots in California and has been following the St. Louis Rams since their days in Los Angeles, California. He lives with his wife Cynthia and recent addition to the team Angelina in Canton, Ohio.